Moving to Florida

Zoraida Rivera
Art by Tanya Lam

Literacy Consultants
David Booth • Kathleen Corrigan

Contents

Chapter 1

A New Place to Live

It's been three boring weeks pacing from room to room. From the window, I look out at all of the boring buildings. Mom, Dad, and I just moved to Florida from Puerto Rico. We're living with my grandparents.

Every morning, Grandpa goes to work at an office, while Mom and Dad go out searching for work. I stay with Grandma.

Every morning, I wonder what to do. It's summertime, but there's no river to swim in or hills to explore as I had back home.

When I close my eyes, I imagine I'm back home hearing the roosters crowing and the birds singing.

Dad decided to move to Florida so that we could be with Grandma.

But I miss our old house. I miss the orange trees, the river, and even eating codfish with green bananas.

At least I'll see my cousin, Lydia, tomorrow. I haven't seen her in a long time. She will be staying with us for two weeks. I'm so excited to see her.

Chapter 2

A Trip Into Town

"Wake up, Sonia! I got up early to come and see you and you're still sleeping," Lydia said, hugging me.

"But there's nothing to do here," I replied, sitting up in bed.

"We'll walk to town," Lydia suggested.

"I already went. It's just boring buildings, streets, and stores," I said sadly.

Lydia frowned.

After breakfast, Lydia and I decided to walk to the supermarket with Grandma. On the walk, Lydia and I lagged behind.

I stared at the apartments. All of the houses seemed glued together. The large buildings and stores seemed like blobs.

"Don't you want to go back to the island?" I asked Lydia.

"Sometimes I miss it. But I like the stores nearby and the crowds here. It's fun seeing all of the different clothes, colors, and languages," Lydia explained.

"Well, I don't like the crowds, streets, or all of these strange sounds. I want to go back home," I replied.

"You might learn to like them. Different things are interesting," said Lydia.

"I won't learn to like them, and I'll never like it here," I insisted.

"Stop it, Sonia!" Lydia exclaimed.

Grandma spun around, her eyes fixed on Lydia. That silenced her. "Just because she's nine doesn't mean she knows more," I thought.

At the supermarket, I didn't talk to Lydia. I started to wonder if living in Florida had changed her.

Chapter 3

Memories of Puerto Rico

I was still angry with Lydia. But deep down, I was glad that she was staying with us. Later that night when we got home, we shared a bed.

"I'm sorry for getting mad at you earlier," Lydia said when I turned off the lights. "I forgot how I felt when I got here. It was October and it was cold! It was even colder than those foggy mornings in Puerto Rico," she said, pulling the sheet over her head.

"But we had the river where we could swim and search for tiny fish. There's nothing like that here," I said sadly.

"Remember all of the castles we built on the beach?" asked Lydia.

"I loved building sand castles," I replied.

"Then at night, we'd listen to the waves and take turns looking for constellations. Here, the city lights hide the stars," Lydia said.

"I can't pick mangoes or oranges from the trees here," I complained. "The town was far away back home and the stores were small, but I loved the hills and the ..." I couldn't speak. Tears came to my eyes.

"When I first got here, I was mad all the time. I hated that everything was new, even the smells," Lydia said.

I was glad Lydia understood what I was feeling.

Chapter 4

A Bit of Hope

Soon Mom found a part-time job, but Dad was still looking for work. He kept telling us to be patient.

Grandpa had found this bigger apartment so that we could all come to Florida. But he can pay for it only for a few months. We all hoped that Dad would find work soon.

The next day, Lydia and I sat at the kitchen table playing cards.

"If Dad doesn't get a job, maybe we'll go back to Puerto Rico," I whispered to Lydia.

"I miss the island too," said Lydia. "But I love being with my family more than I miss Puerto Rico."

After two weeks, Aunt Selma and Uncle Edwin came to visit and to pick up Lydia.

Grandma prepared rice with ham, large red beans, and roasted chicken. We all praised Grandma for her delicious cooking.

I had so much fun with my family that for a little while I forgot I was in Florida.

A few days later, Dad came home and went right to sleep. He kissed my forehead before he went to his room, but he didn't stop to talk to me as he used to. He just let out a deep sigh and walked away.

The night became long, quiet, and dark. After a little while, I heard Dad and Mom whispering fiercely. I hope Dad finds a job soon.

At breakfast the next morning, I stared at Grandma. Remembering Dad's sigh, I wondered what else I didn't know about.

"Grandma, let me do that," I said as she picked up the broom. "You can sit down."

"Me?" Grandma asked. "I don't sit much," she said thoughtfully.

"Why don't we do something you like today?" I asked.

When I finished sweeping, Grandma was ready to go.

"Get ready to walk. We're going out!" I said to her excitedly.

Chapter 5

A Visit With Grandma

We walked the first two blocks toward town, but suddenly Grandma took a different route. The blocks grew larger and the number of houses shrank. There were more places to eat and a few more stores. As the ground became steeper, I began to smile. I saw trees behind a cement wall.

"Where are we going, Grandma? Do they keep nature in a box here?"

"That's a funny way to put it," Grandma said. "The town wants a balance between nature and buildings. The nature in a box is a park."

I didn't understand. Dad used to cut the grass and trim trees back home, but we never kept nature in boxes. I had never been to a park like this in Puerto Rico.

When we got to the park, trees and grass filled my view. There were tiny hills in the distance. Nearby I saw slides and swings. But what caught my attention was a track.

"Can we go there?" I said pointing. Grandma nodded.

I walked on the track while Grandma sat down on a nearby bench.

I walked slow, then fast, and then I jogged. Before long I was running. Soon I didn't see the park. I saw my mountains and heard the familiar sounds of Puerto Rico. The sound of my sneakers on the track was the river water. I ran faster. I was a bird now.

After I ran the length of the track, I went to sit by Grandma. She gave me a hug.

"Wow, you run fast," I heard someone say behind me. I turned around. A girl, who looked about my age, was standing there.

"Hi, I'm Patricia. I run too. I'm on a track team," she said smiling.

"Hi, I'm Sonia. I don't speak English very well, but I speak Spanish," I replied.

"Don't worry. I speak Spanish too," she said, switching to Spanish. "We're having tryouts for our team next week. You should try out. How can you run so fast?" asked Patricia.

"I think about all of the places that I love. It helps me to keep going," I said smiling.

Walking home, I thought about Lydia's words. Lydia was right. Even though things are tough, I love being with my family more than I miss Puerto Rico too.